A TYPICAL ARRANGEMENT OF INSTRUMENTS IN AN ORCHESTRA

THE POSITION OF THE PLAYERS AND
THE SIZE OF THE ORCHESTRA MAY VARY
ACCORDING TO CIRCUMSTANCES.

Series 662

Here is a book which illustrates and describes the various instruments of the orchestra, the brass band and 'pop' group, and also those used for solo playing. It explains how these instruments are played, and how each produces its own individual sound.

This book will introduce children to the orchestra, and add to the pleasure of those already interested in music.

Wherever possible the ranges of the various instruments are shown in relation to the Piano keyboard. In many cases, however, the upper note can vary with the skill of the performer.

A Ladybird Book of
MUSICAL
INSTRUMENTS

by ANN REES, B.Sc.

with illustrations by ROBERT AYTON

Ladybird Books Loughborough

Sounds and how we hear them

All day long we hear sounds. The birds sing, clocks tick, trains whistle and radio and television pour out music. All the sounds that we hear are caused by some kind of *vibration*. When a drummer hits the stretched skin of his drum with a drum-stick, the skin moves backwards and forwards, it vibrates. This movement then makes the air vibrate and waves of sound travel from the drum to our sensitive ears. Our ear-drums pass the vibration through three tiny bones called the hammer, the anvil and the stirrup, to the inner ear. A message about the vibration goes from the inner ear to the brain and we hear the sound.

Musical sounds are produced by regular vibrations and we hear an irregular vibration as a noise. Sound waves cannot pass through an empty space or *vacuum*, but they can travel through air, water or solids. The American Indians used to put their ears to the ground to listen for the enemy.

All musical instruments have a part which vibrates and a hollow sound-box or *resonator* which makes the sound louder. The instruments can be grouped into:

1. Stringed instruments.
2. Wood-wind instruments.
3. Brass instruments.
4. Percussion instruments.
5. Keyboard instruments.

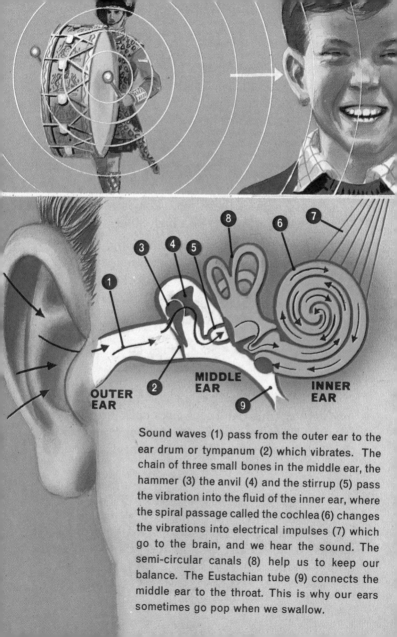

Sound waves (1) pass from the outer ear to the ear drum or tympanum (2) which vibrates. The chain of three small bones in the middle ear, the hammer (3) the anvil (4) and the stirrup (5) pass the vibration into the fluid of the inner ear, where the spiral passage called the cochlea (6) changes the vibrations into electrical impulses (7) which go to the brain, and we hear the sound. The semi-circular canals (8) help us to keep our balance. The Eustachian tube (9) connects the middle ear to the throat. This is why our ears sometimes go pop when we swallow.

Stringed Instruments

All stringed instruments have gut, nylon or wire strings which are stretched and attached to some sort of hollow sound-box. The strings can be vibrated by plucking them, passing a sticky bow over them or by hitting them.

The height or *pitch* of the note that we hear is decided by :

1. The length of the string. Long strings give low notes, short strings give high notes.

2. The tightness or *tension* in the string. If the string is tightened up it plays a higher note. This is how instruments are tuned.

3. The thickness and the weight of the strings. Thick strings are used for the lower notes.

When a string gives out a high note it is vibrating quickly, if it emits a low note it is vibrating slowly.

If a length of string vibrates it plays the main or *fundamental* note, but it also gives out other notes very faintly. These are called overtones, or *harmonics*, and they help to give the different instruments their special tone.

The harp and piano have many strings of different lengths but the violin has only four strings, all of the same length. Extra notes are played by pressing the strings to the fingerboard so that only parts of the strings vibrate.

The Violin and the Viola

The VIOLIN is one of a family of stringed instruments all of which are played with a bow. The violin has four strings of catgut and wire which are stretched along the hollow, wooden body of the instrument. The strings pass from an ebony tailpiece over an upright, wooden bridge, along the ebony fingerboard to four tuning pegs. The strings are tuned to G, D, A, and E. The violinist plays other notes by pressing the strings to the finger-board at certain places so that only parts of the strings vibrate.

The bow is a long piece of springy wood strung with horsehair which is rubbed with a sticky resin. The violinist tucks the violin under his chin, 'stops' the strings with his left hand and vibrates the strings by drawing the sticky bow across them near the bridge. A good violinist can produce many beautiful sounds by using his bow in various ways. Sometimes the strings are plucked with the fingers and this is called 'pizzicato'.

The VIOLA is like a large violin and is also tucked under the chin to be played. Its strings are tuned a fifth lower than the violin to C, G, D and A and it has a deeper tone. The viola usually plays the accompaniment to the main tune.

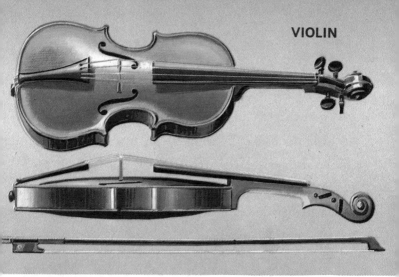

VIOLIN

VIOLIN — VIOLA

MIDDLE C

The Violoncello and the Double-Bass

The VIOLONCELLO or 'CELLO looks like a very large violin, but the 'cellist would find it rather awkward to play if he tucked it under his chin! The 'cello has a spike at the bottom which rests on the floor, while the 'cellist sits down and balances the large hollow body of the instrument between his knees. The 'cello has four strings which are tuned in fifths to C, G, D, and A. The longer strings and the larger body of the 'cello mean a lower pitch of note played. The 'cellist fingers the strings with his left hand and bows the strings with his right hand. The 'cello usually helps to supply the harmony in orchestral music, but it sometimes plays a melody with a beautiful, rich tone.

The DOUBLE-BASS is so large that the player has either to perch on a stool or stand to play it. The strings are very thick and strong so that the double-bass can produce very low notes. The strings are usually tuned in fourths E, A, D, and G. There are about eight double-basses in a symphony orchestra. Pop and jazz groups use the double-bass because the deep notes, which are plucked out, can provide a good rhythm.

The Harp

The HARP is a stringed instrument which is plucked with the fingers. Harps were played in ancient Egypt and the instrument is mentioned in the Bible. The modern harp is almost triangular in shape, and it is strung with about forty-five strings each of different length and thickness, some made of gut and some of wire. The strings are attached to a sound-box on one side of the triangle and stretch across the harp to metal tuning pegs. There are so many strings to tune that the harpist is usually in the concert hall long before the rest of the orchestra. The harpist sits down and pulls the harp towards her so that it rests on one shoulder and she plucks the strings with her fingers. The pitch of the strings can also be changed with foot pedals. Sometimes the harpist runs her fingers quickly over all the strings to give a rippling effect which is called *glissando*. Harps are usually very beautifully carved.

The Welsh and Irish bards used to sing with small harps called Gaelic harps. These had fewer strings and were easy to carry around. Some folk-singers still use the Gaelic harp to accompany their songs.

HARP

The Guitar

Folk-singers and Pop-groups have helped to make the GUITAR a popular instrument again. Guitars similar to those played today were known in Spain in the 16th century and the Spanish type of guitar is still used. The strings of the guitar are plucked and the finger-board has metal strips, called frets, set into it at intervals. The player presses the strings down on the finger-board behind the required frets so that only a part of each string vibrates. The six strings of the guitar are tuned to E, A, D, G, B, E . The strings of the highest pitch are made of gut or nylon, the others are made of fine silk or nylon covered with thin, coiled, silver wire. The strings pass from tuning pegs, along the finger-board to a flat bridge near the round sound-hole of the instrument. The guitar player can sit or stand to play, he fingers with the left hand and plucks the strings with his right hand.

The ELECTRIC GUITAR is similar to the Spanish guitar. Usually it has six strings but the vibrations of the plucked string are not magnified by a hollow, wooden body but by an electric amplifier and a speaker.

SPANISH GUITAR

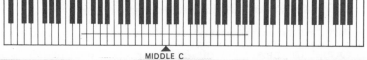

GUITAR

MIDDLE C

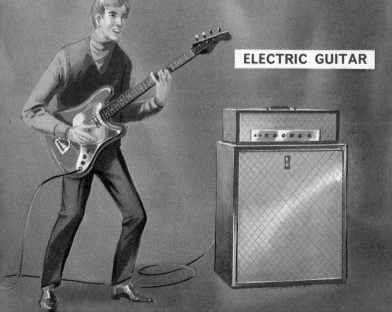

ELECTRIC GUITAR

The Mandoline, the Lute and the Banjo

The MANDOLINE is an instrument, shaped like a small lute, which came from Italy. The LUTE is an old instrument with a pear-shaped body and many strings. It was used by the minstrels and singers but it was rather delicate and difficult to play. The mandoline has only four pairs of strings which are tuned to the same notes as the violin. The player fingers the strings on the fretted finger-board with his left hand and with his right hand he plucks the strings, using a piece of bone or metal called a *plectrum*. The instrument has a round sound-hole. All but the shortest notes are produced by a rapid to and fro movement of the plectrum. This gives a vibrating quality to the sound of the mandoline.

The BANJO is often played in jazz and pop-groups and it was used to accompany Negro folk-songs. The instrument has a fretted finger-board, but the hollow sound-box is made from a piece of wood covered by a sheet of parchment which is stretched over a wooden hoop. The banjo can have metal or gut strings and it can be played in different ways, with the fingers or with a plectrum. It can also have four or five strings tuned to different sets of notes.

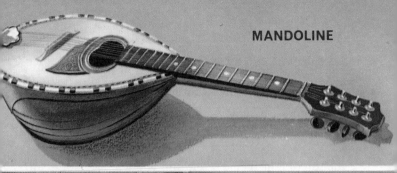

MANDOLINE

BANJO

MANDOLINE • G BANJO

MIDDLE C

Wind Instruments

Wood-wind and brass instruments produce music when the player blows into them in some way. Air which is enclosed in a pipe or metal tube can be made to vibrate and give out a musical note. Try blowing across the top of a medicine bottle and you will hear some sort of musical tone. The pitch of the note depends on the volume of air in the bottle. If water is poured into the bottle so that there is less air to vibrate, the bottle plays a higher note. A long tube of vibrating air plays a low note, a short tube plays a high note. The air is vibrated in different ways in the various instruments, by blowing across a hole, through a mouthpiece, or by making the lips vibrate.

Some instruments have a number of holes in the tube of wood or metal. If all the holes are covered with the fingers the whole length of air in the tube will vibrate, but if some of the holes are uncovered, only a part of the air will vibrate. In brass instruments, valves and other devices are used to open up or close off extra lengths of tubing.

Pipes and Recorders

For thousands of years, men have played music on pipes made from hollow bamboo or wood. Since long tubes play low notes and short tubes play high notes, tubes of different lengths were tied together to produce an instrument called the pan-pipes. A number of notes could also be played on a single tube or pipe which had several holes in it. In the BAGPIPES, air is blown into a bag which is then tucked under the player's arm. When the bag is squeezed, air is forced through a few pipes to produce a droning tune.

You have probably heard or even played a RECORDER. It is an old instrument which is often used today. The recorder is a wooden tube with six or seven finger-holes in it. The player blows into a mouthpiece and a stream of air passes over a sharp edge. This disturbs the air, it vibrates and gives out a note whose pitch depends on the length of air in the pipe. Other notes are played by fingering the holes. Of the four recorders shown the descant plays the highest notes. When very high notes are required a smaller instrument called a sopranino recorder is used.

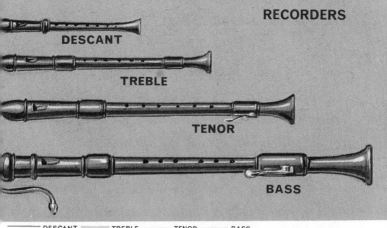

RECORDERS

DESCANT

TREBLE

TENOR

BASS

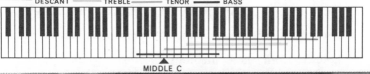

DESCANT   TREBLE   TENOR   BASS

MIDDLE C

The Piccolo and the Flute

The PICCOLO and the FLUTE are members of the wood-wind family of the orchestra. Some flutes are made of wood although a few are also made of silver. The flute is a straight pipe with holes bored in it, and the flautist (or flute player) holds the instrument to the right of his face and blows across a hole at one end of the flute. The flautist can control the type of sound that he produces by changing the position of his lips. The holes in the flute are opened and closed by pressing down metal keys; in the recorder, the fingers themselves cover up the holes. Both these methods of fingering change the length of the vibrating air column. The flute can produce beautiful, rippling melodies but its lower notes are not as strong as the higher notes.

The PICCOLO is a short little flute which has the highest pitch of all the instruments in the orchestra. It is played in the same way as the flute and it has a penetrating tone. There is one other flute called the BASS FLUTE which is not often used but it can produce a low tone. In an orchestra the flautist may be required to play any of these instruments.

PICCOLO

FLUTE

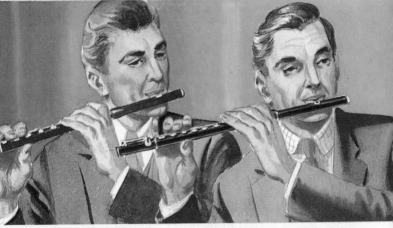

PICCOLO — FLUTE

MIDDLE C

The Oboe and the Cor Anglais

The OBOE has a beautiful, penetrating tone. The instrument was originally played in France in the seventeenth century and it is now an important instrument in the wood-wind section of the orchestra. The oboe is a wooden pipe about two feet long which opens out into a small bell at the bottom. There are holes at intervals along this pipe which can be opened or closed by the oboe player pressing down metal keys, as on the flute. The vibration is started by the oboe player who blows in a special way through the mouthpiece called a double reed. Two pieces of reed or bamboo are bound around a small metal tube, leaving a small space between the reeds at the other end where they are placed between the player's lips. The oboe is the instrument which usually plays an A to help all the players in the orchestra to tune their instruments correctly. An old type of oboe which is sometimes heard is the OBOE D'AMORE. The COR ANGLAIS is an instrument which is similar to the oboe and is played in the same way but it has a lower tone.

COR ANGLAIS

OBOE

OBOE — COR ANGLAIS

MIDDLE C

The Clarinet

The CLARINET was invented in Germany at the beginning of the eighteenth century. It is an important member of the wood-wind family of the orchestra and has a rich tone. The clarinet is a tube of wood with holes which are covered or uncovered by metal keys as in most other wood-wind instruments. The lower end of the clarinet flares out into a bell shape.

The clarinet mouthpiece has a single cane reed which is attached to the top of the instrument where there is an opening in the tube. The player produces a musical note by compressing his lips into a special shape which is called an *embouchure*.

The pitch of the note played by an oboe or a clarinet depends on the length and shape of the tube of vibrating air and on the shape of the player's lips.

The BASS CLARINET is similar to the clarinet but it plays a lower range of notes. Most clarinets are tuned in B flat or in A. The clarinet is a versatile instrument and is used in many jazz groups.

CLARINET

B flat CLARINET — BASS CLARINET

MIDDLE C

The Bassoon and the Saxophone

The BASSOON is a type of oboe which can play very low notes. The tube of the bassoon is about eight feet long and this explains why the instrument plays notes which are about two octaves lower than those of the oboe. The tube is doubled back on itself to make the instrument easier to hold and carry around. The bassoon has a double reed, similar to that of the oboe, which is at the end of a curved tube. The bassoon player holds the instrument at an angle in front of his body so that the widest end of the bassoon points up in the air. The DOUBLE BASSOON, which has an even lower tone than the bassoon, is sixteen feet long and is bent back on itself four times.

The SAXOPHONE was invented by a fine clarinettist called Sax. It has a mouthpiece with a reed like that of the clarinet, but is made from a wide metal tube which ends in a curved horn shape. Therefore the instrument resembles both wood-wind and brass instruments. It is sometimes used in the orchestra, but it is more often found in dance and jazz bands. There are soprano, alto, tenor, baritone and bass saxophones which produce various ranges of notes.

BASSOON

SAXOPHONE

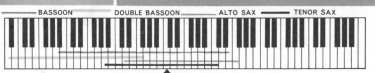

BASSOON — DOUBLE BASSOON — ALTO SAX — TENOR SAX

MIDDLE C

The French Horn

Many years ago, shepherds and huntsmen used to blow into the hollowed-out horns of animals. Then men found that they could make similar horns from metal. These were the beginnings of all the brass instruments in a modern orchestra. If a long column of air in a metal tube is made to vibrate it will produce a note, the longer the tube the lower the note. Different notes are played on a straight hunting-horn if the player changes the pressure of his lips. With tight lips a high note is played, with his lips loose he plays a lower note.

The orchestral or FRENCH HORN is descended from the hunting-horn. It is made from a length of brass tube (about twelve feet long) which is coiled into a complicated shape to make the instrument portable. The length of tube can be changed by pressing down combinations of valves which bring extra lengths of tubing into use. A range of notes can be obtained by change of lip pressure on the funnel-shaped mouthpiece and by pressing down the valves. The tone of the French horn can also be affected when the player puts his hand in the wide bell of the instrument.

FRENCH HORN

FRENCH HORN

MIDDLE C

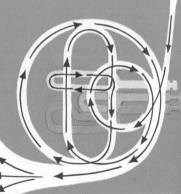

Sound waves vibrating in the long length of brass tubing of the horn. On the diagram the yellow valve is pressed down which brings the extra length of tubing into use.

The Trumpet, the Cornet and the Bugle

From the earliest times, the trumpet has been used to call soldiers to battle. The modern trumpet is made of a brass tube which is about five feet long, and for convenience the tube is bent back on itself. There is a cup-shaped mouthpiece at one end of the instrument and a bell shape at the other. In the old trumpets, the length of the instruments was fixed, the pitch of the note was changed with the lips and the number of possible notes was small. In the modern trumpet the length of tube can be altered by pressing down combinations of three valves. This brings in extra lengths of tubing. A piece of hollow wood or leather called a *mute* is sometimes put in the bell end of the trumpet to change the sound given out. Trumpets are used in orchestras, jazz bands and brass bands.

The CORNET is a smaller version of the trumpet which is sometimes used in the orchestra but it is mainly found in brass bands.

The BUGLE is a trumpet which has no valves and a limited number of notes. The bugle player in the army has various bugle calls which are used on different occasions.

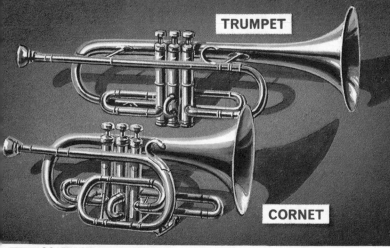

TRUMPET

CORNET

B flat TRUMPET   CORNET

MIDDLE C

The Tuba and the Trombone

The TUBA is one of a family of instruments called the Saxhorns. The tuba and the EUPHONIUM are both bass saxhorns which are tuned to different notes. The tuba is the largest orchestral instrument made from brass, and plays very low notes. It is held so that the large bell at one end points up into the air. The player obtains all the notes by using his mouth and by pressing combinations of four or five valves.

The TROMBONE is a brass instrument which is played in orchestras, brass bands, and jazz bands. The trombone has a long tube which is bent into an oblong shape for convenience, and this tube flares into a bell shape at one end. The mouthpiece is cup-shaped, and the length of the tube is changed by a movable loop of brass which is called the *slide*. The trombone player can play all the notes in the scale by changing his lip pressure, or *embouchure*, and by moving the slide in and out. The trombonist can get some amusing effects by moving the slide rapidly and blowing at the same time. There is also a BASS TROMBONE with a lower range than the normal trombone.

TUBA

TROMBONE — BASS TROMBONE — TUBA

MIDDLE C

TROMBONE

The Kettle Drums or Timpani,
the Bass Drum and the Side Drum

All percussion instruments are struck in some way to produce sounds, the most familiar probably being the drums. All the drums have parchment or skin stretched over some type of frame and they are usually hit with drumsticks.

The KETTLE DRUMS or TIMPANI can be tuned to play notes of a different pitch by tightening the skin which is stretched across the large copper bowls which act as resonators. Padded drumsticks are used to hit the drum. During a concert the drummer can often be seen tuning his timpani by turning taps on the rims of the drums.

The BASS DRUM is the largest of the drums, and is a shallow wooden shell covered on both sides with stretched parchment. It is played with one or two large padded drumsticks and is held or placed in an upright position. Jazz drummers beat the bass drum by pressing down a foot pedal which works the drumstick.

The SIDE DRUM is a smaller horizontal version of the bass drum and is played with small wooden-headed drumsticks. Catgut strings called snares, are stretched across the lower parchment and make a rattling noise. Jazz and pop drummers use a number of different side drums.

KETTLE DRUMS

BASS DRUM

SIDE DRUM

The Tambourine, Castanets, Triangle, Block and Rattle

The TAMBOURINE is a small, light hoop of wood which has pairs of loose metal discs let into it. Skin is stretched across one side of the hoop and the instrument is played by tapping the skin with the fingers or the knuckles. It can also be shaken vigorously to make the metal pieces rattle. Spanish gypsies use the tambourine when they dance.

The CASTANETS are also used by Spanish dancers. They are two shell-shaped pieces of hard wood which are strung together, held in the hand and clicked together. The castanets in the orchestra are strung on a handle for convenience.

The TRIANGLE is made from a metal rod which has been bent into a triangular shape that is open at one corner. The triangle is held suspended by the player while he taps it with another metal rod. It gives out a small tinkling noise which can be heard quite clearly amongst the other instruments.

The BLOCK is a piece of wood which is hit to produce a sharp noise.

A RATTLE which is sometimes used in the orchestra is rather like the rattles used by enthusiastic football supporters.

TAMBOURINE

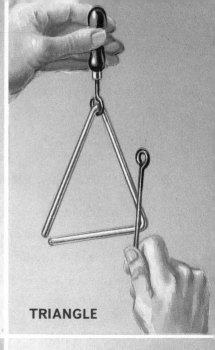

TRIANGLE

CASTANETS

WOOD BLOCK

The Tubular Bells, Xylophone, Cymbals and Gong

The TUBULAR BELLS. If a tube is hit, it will give out a note which depends on its length. A long tube will give out a low note and a short tube produces a high note. The tubular bells are a row of tubes of different lengths which are strung up on a rack.

The XYLOPHONE is made from a number of wooden bars of different lengths which are fixed horizontally on a frame. The bars are hit with small padded hammers. Underneath each bar is a metal tube which acts as a resonator.

The CYMBALS are large circular discs of brass with leather handles at the centre. The player can make a wonderful crashing noise by hitting them against each other. Sometimes one cymbal is balanced so that the drummer can hit it with his drumstick. Jazz drummers use the cymbal in this way. The cymbals are often used in exciting music.

The GONG is a very large piece of metal which is shaped rather like a tin lid. The player hits the gong with a large drumstick with a padded head. The gong gives out a loud booming noise.

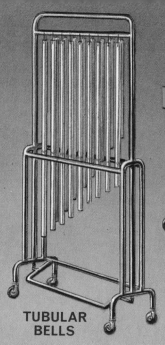

TUBULAR BELLS

XYLOPHONE

THE GONG

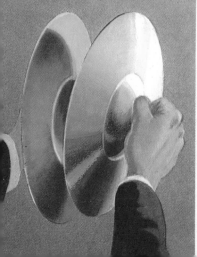

CYMBALS

The Dulcimer, Glockenspiel, Celeste and Zither

The DULCIMER works like a small piano. It has a soundboard with a number of stretched strings which are hit with small wooden hammers. This instrument is often found in the percussion section of the orchestra.

The GLOCKENSPIEL is made from a number of metal plates each of different length, each plate thus giving out a different note. The metal bars are struck with a pair of small hammers. The instrument gives out a pretty chiming note.

The CELESTE is a special type of glockenspiel but it has a keyboard and looks like a small piano. The celeste has a number of metal plates which are fixed to hollow, wooden resonators which produce a fairylike tone. The keys work small hammers which make the plates vibrate.

The ZITHER is a very old stringed instrument which has a hollow, flat sound-box and about thirty to forty strings. There are frets on the fingerboard which help the player to 'stop' the strings, and the fingers are used to pluck the strings.

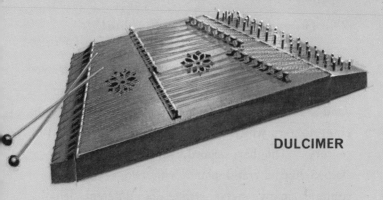

DULCIMER

GLOCKENSPIEL

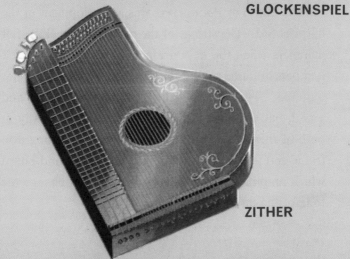

ZITHER

The Harpsichord, Spinet, Virginal, Clavichord and Piano

Most instruments with a keyboard are stringed instruments, for example, the piano, but the organ is a wind instrument. The piano is a descendant of the HARPSICHORD which was popular from the 16th to 18th century. The harpsichord, which is still played, is shaped like a grand piano with two keyboards and contains many metal strings of different lengths, each tuned to a different note. When the player presses down a key, a system of levers work and one of the strings in the harpsichord is plucked by a quill and vibrates. The SPINET and the VIRGINAL are similar instruments. In the CLAVICHORD the strings are hit by small pieces of metal.

The PIANO or PIANOFORTE was a development of the harpsichord. The strings of the piano are struck by felt hammers when the keys are pressed down. Small felt dampers are used to stop the strings vibrating when not required. There are two kinds of piano, upright and grand, but the sound is produced in a similar way in both of them. The strings are strung on a strong iron frame and in both types of piano there is a sound-board which amplifies the sound. The pedals can change the tone of the instrument.

HARPSICHORD

UPRIGHT PIANO

HARPSICHORD — PIANO

▲
MIDDLE C

The Organ

The ORGAN is the largest of all the instruments and it can produce a wonderful volume of sound. Most organs are built into churches and concert halls.

The organ has a large number of pipes of different sizes, the long pipes give out the low notes and the short pipes emit high notes. Some pipes, called flue pipes, look rather like enormous tin whistles, others, which produce quite a different kind of sound, are known as reed pipes because the sound is made when a reed vibrates, as in the clarinet or oboe. Although handblown instruments may still be found, most organs today are blown by powerful electric fans.

The organ has keyboards, called manuals, which are played with the hands and a keyboard, consisting of pedals, which is worked by the feet. The organist uses controls called 'stops' to produce the tone he wants. When a key is pressed, air enters one or more of the pipes and vibrates to give out the required sound.

Electronic organs, which have loudspeakers instead of pipes, are now quite common. These are usually quite small but they, too, can produce a great variety and volume of sound.

The Human Voice

The HUMAN VOICE is probably the most wonderful of all the instruments and yet we take it for granted. Most people can sing tunes quite easily when they are young, and some people have very good voices which they practise at using in the same way as a pianist practises at the piano.

The human voice is rather like a wood-wind instrument. When you sing you must first take in a deep breath to fill your lungs with air. In your throat there are membranes called the vocal cords which are contained within the voice box or larynx. When you think of a note to sing, these cords are subconsciously tightened to a certain tension and air is blown over them from your lungs. The vocal cords are set into vibration and give out a certain note. This sound is made a good deal louder in the hollow spaces in the mouth, cheeks and throat.

Singers must practise for a long time to obtain good control of their breathing and to be able to pitch their notes accurately.

Diagram on the left shows the vocal cords in the larynx tensioned to form a narrow slit through which air is forced. The vocal cords vibrate producing a sound which is made louder in the cavities of the head and throat. We adjust the tension to make a higher or lower note. The diagram on the right shows the vocal cords in a relaxed open position as we breathe.

The Conductor and the Orchestra

Musical instruments can be combined in many ways. There are brass and military bands, jazz and pop-groups, but probably the best way to hear many instruments playing together is to listen to an orchestra.

The LEADER of the orchestra is the principal first violinist, and he assists the CONDUCTOR. The Conductor is an important person, because he ensures that the sounds of all the instruments in the various sections— the strings, woodwind, brass and percussion—are blended together so that the music is played according to the wishes of the composer. He reads the music from a large SCORE, and with a small stick, called a BATON, he indicates the correct beat. With this baton—and with a nod, a flicker of an eyelid or the movement of a finger— his powers seem almost magical as the orchestra responds with magnificent sound or the quietest of whispers. Sometimes he controls a hundred players— and even a choir and soloists as well!

Many rehearsals are, of course, necessary before a concert is given or a recording made, but during all these the Conductor is helping each musician to perfect his contribution.

There are many things in this world that compete for our attention, but the present day perfection of broadcasting and recording is helping more and more people to become aware of the pleasure that great music can add to their lives.

INDEX

	Page			Page
Banjo - - -	16	Lute - - -		16
Bassoon - - -	28	Mandoline - -		16
Bass Clarinet - -	26			
Bass Drum - -	36	Oboe - - -		24
Block - - -	38	Oboe D'amore -		24
Bugle - - -	32	Organ - - -		46
Castanets - -	38	Piano - - -		44
Celeste - - -	42	Piccolo - - -		22
Clarinet - - -	26	Pipes - - -		20
Clavichord - -	44			
Conductor - -	50	Rattle - - -		38
Cor Anglais - -	24	Recorders - -		20
Cornet - - -	32			
Cymbals - - -	40	Saxophone - -		28
		Side Drum - -		36
Double Bass - -	10	Spinet - - -		44
Dulcimer - - -	42			
		Tambourine - -		38
Euphonium - -	34	Triangle - - -		38
		Trombone - -		34
Flute - - -	22	Trumpet - - -		32
French Horn - -	30	Tuba - - -		34
		Tubular Bells - -		40
Glockenspiel - -	42			
Gong - - -	40	Viola - - -		8
Guitar - - -	14	Violin - - -		8
		Violoncello - -		10
Harp - - -	12	Virginal - - -		44
Harpsichord - -	44			
Human Voice - -	48	Xylophone - -		40
Kettle Drums		Zither - - -		42
(or Timpani) -	36			